# Jump-Starting Your Devotional Life

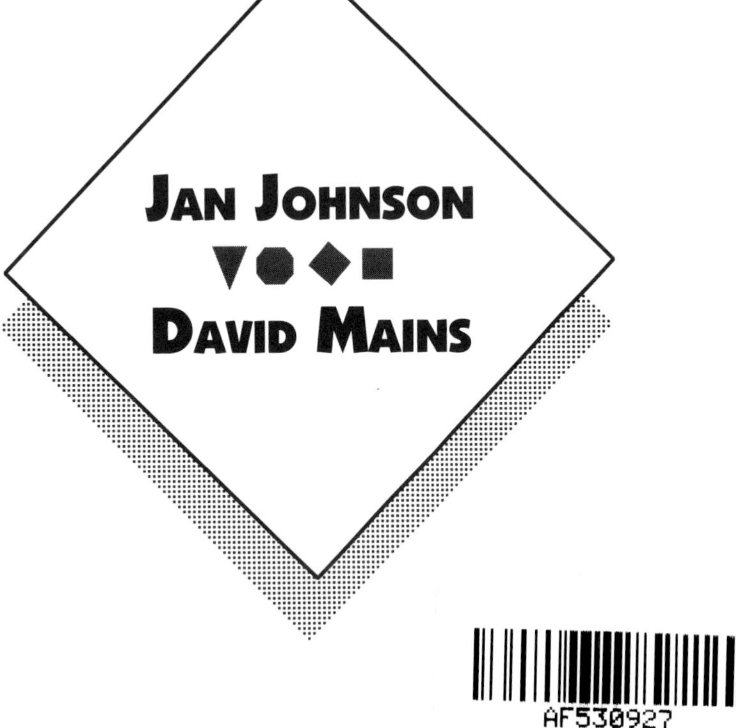




David C. Cook Publishing Co. Elgin, Illinois—Weston, Ontario

Jump-Starting Your Devotional Life



Published by David C. Cook Publishing Co.
850 North Grove Ave., Elgin, IL 60120
Cable address: DCCOOK
Designed by Randy Maid
Cover illustration by Guy Wolek
Inside illustrations by Bruce Van Patter
Printed in U.S.A.

ISBN: 1-55513-376-2

# CONTENTS

# ARE YOU READY FOR A CHRISTIAN LIFESTYLE?

Ever noticed that you can swim along for years in the Christian life without leaving the shallow end of the pool? Then one day it hits you: If you're going to *do* anything about your faith, you've got to go deeper. If you're going to have a truly satisfying walk with God, you've got to plunge past surface spirituality, empty words, faith without action.

But you're wary. What will a really *Christian* lifestyle be like? Will you have to overcommit yourself? Will God demand the impossible of you? Will you have to erase your personality and become a musty, dusty saint from the pre-TV, pre-stereo, pre-microwave days?

## Commitment for Today's Adults

Wary—that's how many of today's adults feel when they're urged to be "on fire for the Lord." They want to turn faith to action, but they've been raised to ask themselves, "What's in it for me?" They want to get serious about the Christian life—but in a new-fashioned way that works for them.

That's why we've introduced The Christian Lifestyle Series. It's designed to help today's adults "get real" about their commitment to Christ. Each course nudges them toward becoming more consistent disciples—without browbeating or boring them. Each session helps them to be honest about their struggles and take realistic, workable steps toward greater faithfulness.

## Sessions for Today's Groups

Whether you lead a large Sunday school class or a small group, you know that today's adults hate five things:

- Boring lectures
- Lots of homework
- Being told what to think
- Subjects that have nothing to do with their everyday lives; and
- Courses that seem to go on forever.

The Christian Lifestyle Series lightens the load of lecture and increases active group participation. Each course offers reproducible student Resource sheets instead of requiring group members to read time-consuming, expensive student books. Each session asks for and respects group members' contributions and emphasizes real-life application. And instead of lasting twelve or thirteen weeks, each course wraps up in seven. If you want to fit a quarterly thirteen-week format, just combine two courses and skip the introductory session in one of them.

## Format for Today's Leaders

Because you're busy, these sessions are easy to prepare and use. The step-by-step plans are easy to follow; instructions to the leader are in regular type, things you might say aloud are in bold type, and suggested answers are in parentheses.

A helpful article introduces the course, giving you an overview of the topic. The reproducible student Resource sheets are meant to be photocopied and handed out—or turn some into overhead projector transparencies if you like. Most sessions include a Resource sheet that will help prepare group members for your next meeting, too.

As always, feel free to adapt this course to the needs of your group. And may God use these sessions to help your group members discover the joy of a truly Christian lifestyle.

*John Duckworth, Series Editor*

# YOUR GROUP AND THE DEVOTIONAL LIFE

*By David Mains*

Sitting in my first weight-loss class, I was quickly aware that everyone around the table had more pounds than needed. Everyone, that is, except one person—the instructor. She was trim, attractive, well-dressed, and obviously feeling quite good about her appearance. I found myself having trouble with her teaching style; I made mental notes of her grammatical errors and rationalized that she knew nothing of the pressures of my schedule.

Then, about halfway through the first session, she confessed that she used to weigh almost twice what she did now. She testified to having tried many weight-loss methods, but all of them had failed. She told about her problems with bulimia. She described how she finally had happened upon the approach to weight loss she was now teaching. It worked wonderfully well and she was truly excited about it!

On top of that, she was convinced all of us could achieve the same level of success she had. When I heard those words it was the first time I felt as though I had come to the right place.

## A Place to Be Honest

Leading a group in a study about the devotional life, you can assume that almost everyone attending is spiritually flabby. Part of this is because most people have an unreal mental picture of what a person with a strong devotional life really is. In their minds it means rising early every morning and spending at least twenty to thirty minutes reading the Bible and then having an intimate prayer time during which the Lord reveals Himself in all His glory. Most of your students will have heard quotes about various leaders of the church who spent so many hours on their knees that the caps began to look like they belonged to camels!

But none of this information will do much more than build barriers between you and your group members, until it's openly admitted that this is a very difficult topic and most people have trouble trying to make it work. It might be better to begin by letting them identify with your failures rather than your successes.

What would Christ say about His expectations regarding the devotional lives of your group members? What would He say about mine? If He were introducing me as group leader, I have a feeling He would say that I'm strong in certain devotional aspects and weak in others. But I also sense He would say that in my honesty He would see me as a good leader, and would expect that I could draw from the group that which would be helpful to all.

The way in which I think He would introduce me is how I should view myself in this leading role—nothing more, nothing less. The same should be true for you. Don't pretend to be something you aren't.

## Jump-Starts and Long Hauls

*Jump-Starting Your Devotional Life* . . . That's an interesting title, isn't it? I like the way it's phrased. Many times a simple spiritual charge can bring new life to numerous aspects of your walk with the Lord.

For example, victory over a temptation of long standing can do wonders for your prayer life. Setting up an accountability relationship with a fellow Christian can motivate you to get up early when otherwise you might sleep in. Buying a new translation of the Bible or purchasing a Bible dictionary can open up parts of Scripture that before were difficult for you. Having a quiet time alone once a week with your wife or one of your children or a friend can be an added incentive to meet privately with the Lord. There are many ways to put a charge into your devotional life apart from an extensive overhauling of your spiritual engine. And spiritual "jumper cables" really are available that relate to the topic at hand.

Be aware, however, that for a person to know any measure of success in his or her devotional life, time must be given to it. Even the best ideas won't work if they are never tried!

When our lives are busy, which they are, it's necessary to set priorities. This way the necessary attention can be given to the chosen subject. Never forget that the word devotion has synonyms such as commitment, attentiveness, devoutness, piety, and spirituality. None of these is cultivated without establishing some kind of priority timewise.

## Share Simple, Practical Tips

In Christ's life, "devotions" often meant having to get up a great while before the day began. That also probably meant He went to bed earlier than most people. This has certainly been the case for me in my life. I can't consistently get up early if I'm always getting to bed late.

As simple as it sounds, that's a great secret to share. Being alert when with the Lord in the morning means learning to end social relationships earlier than most people do. You won't make a habit of watching the late news. You have to learn when to stop reading or working on the project of the moment because of the important early appointment the following day.

The devotional life also relates to the matter of finding quiet. We live in a noisy world. Personally, I find it extremely difficult to have quality time with the Lord when I'm hearing something distracting. That's why on occasion I will go to the office to be alone, or take a ride in the car when I want to pray and my kids have friends over. Or I tell others in the house that I prefer not to be the one who answers the phone for the next thirty minutes because I'm taking some time to meet with the Lord.

The best of thoughts regarding meditation or Scripture study or intercessory prayer are of little value to someone if a roommate or the person in the next apartment is playing rock music on the stereo. In other words, don't let your group drift into spiritual platitudes while overlooking more immediate, practical problems.

Let me pursue this further. As a leader, don't hesitate to share what to you may seem the most simple suggestions. Recently I talked with a friend who said he had trouble praying because as soon as he started all kinds of thoughts came into his mind. Some of them were quite good. But before long he found himself having trouble trying to remember everything. Pretty soon his thinking became so befuddled it brought his praying to a screeching halt.

I shared that I always pray with a notepad and a pencil. That's because I regularly have the same experience. When I'm praying, the Lord often brings things to mind that need to be done, or excellent suggestions regarding solutions to problems. It's not unusual for me to get broadcast ideas in the middle of a prayer time.

The way I keep my mind clear is to write these thoughts down. Then I don't have to try to keep them all in my head. In fact, I often begin praying expecting God to answer questions for me, because this is when I sense that He is very close. I don't believe it offends Him that I bring a pencil and paper to our times together.

Now this is hardly a profound idea to share, is it? But I heard from the same person that it was a tremendous help to him. It's giving him a whole new freedom in his prayer life.

The importance of this study is not going to depend on whether everything you share is a "deep spiritual truth." The key is whether or not you're helping pull off the specified objective—namely, helping those who attend to have a more meaningful devotional life.

## Set Attainable Goals

With this in mind, in your preparation think in terms of simplicity rather than profundity. This includes making small steps of success your objective rather than expecting group members to become viable candidates for the "saint of the year" award.

One of the more common problems defeating people in their spiritual walk is that ministers and teachers tend to hold up an ideal that's far beyond what any of them can accomplish. A pastor shares from a position of privilege. He usually has his own office, a secretary, and an income is paid him to be "spiritual." It's quite another thing for a young mother with three children and little privacy to match spiritually what he is experiencing. For her, small, attainable goals are very important.

So it was in the weight-loss class, where it was always of benefit when each of us could share simple successes. "I lost two pounds this week." "I broke the pattern of stopping for donuts on my way to work." "I didn't snack after ten o'clock even once this last week."

One day Jesus was praying in a place where He apparently went quite often. When He was finished, His disciples—probably highly intimidated—said, "Lord, teach us to pray the way You do."

The response our Lord gave was extremely simple. "When you pray, do it this way." The thoughts that followed were elementary. They related to worship, one of the themes you'll be exploring in this course; to advancing His kingship; to asking God to meet our daily needs; to making sure our relationships are right; and to asking for aid against our spiritual enemy. The prayer wasn't more than what the disciples could handle at the moment.

Your group of disciples (that word means students of a teacher) should be able to let you know whether or not you are over their heads. Hopefully you, too, will be right on target in terms of what they feel they can handle.

## Not Perfect, but Running

I believe all the subtopics in this course are well chosen. Some are more traditional; others, such as journaling, might appear to some to be novel. But all of these are time-honored methods of keeping people on track spiritually.

When a car is jump-started, it means that's it's running again. It doesn't mean the oil has been changed, or the plugs replaced. But it is operating. Work may still need to be done on balancing the wheels or adjusting the transmission. Possibly it still has rust problems and maybe the windshield wipers need to be replaced. But the car is running.

In the short time frame of this course, that's the objective: To see to it that the spiritual life is running once again. It's hard to "run" without some kind of devotional life. Other problems may need attention, but at least you can turn the key and drive from one place to another.

If the members of your group sense that they are once again moving spiritually, you will have accomplished a great thing! The joy and the relief they will know will be major. As time goes on, they'll take care of other matters that need to be attended to. But they will be no longer stalled; they will be moving forward!

"Thanks a lot." That's what motorists say when they get a jump-start. If you help as I've suggested, I believe your group members will say this to you as well.

# WHY DO I FEEL SO SLEEPY?

## Fears and Frustrations of the Devotional Life

Devotions: Are they a chore, a delight, a mystery, or an impossible dream?

This course, and especially this session, will help your group members clear out their preconceived notions about devotions. It will eliminate the rules of devotions and stress the *relationship* involved. It will also help people figure out where they stand with their devotional lives and air some of their feelings about that. Don't be alarmed if some of those feelings are negative. They reveal a desire to be close to God that hasn't been fulfilled.

Think about yourself and your group members:

Some wonder what devotions are all about. They hear the pastor talk about them, but they don't know what a "quiet time" is.

Others have tried devotions a few times and experienced a few successes, but also some confusion.

Still others have struggled to have consistent personal devotions. They've used daily devotional books or even read-through-the-Bible-in-a-year programs. It's been a discouraging cycle: They enjoy; they falter; they quit. Then they start up again. It gets almost embarrassing to come before God and say, "Here I am again, Lord. Remember me?"

Perhaps you have still others who have given up the whole idea of devotions, or who have always thought devotions unnecessary.

And then there are those who have struggled with their devotional lives and have found something that nurtures them. If you know such believers, ask them to share their experiences with your group during this course.

### Where You're Headed:

To help your group members trust God to build their devotional lives, and to cast off misunderstood "rules" and negative feelings about spending time alone with God.

### Scriptures You'll Apply:

Mark 1:21-37; II Peter 1:3-9

### Things You'll Need:

- Bibles
- Chalkboard and chalk or newsprint and marker
- Copies of Resource 1, "Quiet Time Quandaries"
- Resource 2, "What's Your Type?" copied as a transparency or as handouts
- Copies of Resource 3, "I Knew God Loved Me When . . ." (optional)
- Overhead projection equipment (optional)

## 1 Emotions and Devotions

(5-10 minutes)

Expressing Our Feelings about "Having Devotions"

If your group members like to hang around your meeting room and talk before the session begins, try writing these two sentences on the chalkboard or newsprint before the session:

"Personal devotions are important because . . ."

"Personal devotions are a problem because . . ."

As people arrive, give them pieces of chalk and ask them to finish both of the sentences. After several people have done so, begin the session.

Ask: **When I say "devotions," what do you think of?**

Listen to replies, which may include a mix of positives, negatives, and frustrations. If you used the optional opener, read the answers from the chalkboard or newsprint and add them as examples.

**Let's make sure we all have the same definition of "devotions" in mind. For the purposes of this course, devotions are times in which people get to know God. These times usually involve prayer and Bible reading in some way. Let's see how you relate to that personally.**

Pass out copies of Resource 1, "Quiet Time Quandaries," to each group member. Call the group's attention to Part I. Read together the three anecdotes about Jeff, Kathy, and Dave.

**Which of these examples is most like your present or past attitude toward devotions?**

Ask students to explain their choices. If you have more than ten participants, you might form small groups and ask them to share this information with each other.

## 2 What's Your Type?

(5-10 minutes)

Understanding Common Responses to the Devotional Challenge

Display Resource 2, "What's Your Type?" on an overhead projector—or just hand out copies. You might introduce it this way:

**There's an old saying that there are three kinds of people: those who make things happen, those who watch things happen, and those who wonder what happened. You might say there are three kinds of Christians who feel uneasy about their devotional lives. We'll call them the Uptight, the Slow-moving, and the Confused.**

As you make the following comments, point out the appropriate parts of the sheet if you're using an overhead projector.

**The Uptight:**

**These Christians don't just make things happen—they *force* them to happen. They expect to have a mature devotional life before they've grown into it. They may force themselves to rise at 4:00 A.M., read a dozen chapters in the 29-pound family Bible, and run through an 18-page prayer list—even if all they get out of it is eyestrain. If they miss a chapter or a prayer request, they feel guilty. If they miss a day, they fear for their lives. That was Jeff's problem.** Refer back to Jeff's example on Resource 1.

**The Slow-moving:**

**These Christians think about having devotions, but rarely try. In their defense, it should be said that devotions can be a pretty**

**challenging undertaking.** Refer to the Kathy example.

**The Confused:**

**These Christians try to follow all the rules they've heard about "devotions" and come away confused. They keep looking for a mystical formula to help them. After reading a chapter from the Bible, they often think, "So, was that it?"** Refer to the example of Dave.

**Of course, there's a fourth group that isn't listed. It includes those who have worked on their devotional lives and believe those lives are growing. Their devotional lives nurture them in their faith and help them know and relate to God.** If you're displaying the sheet, draw a stick figure or a check mark in the unbuilt house to show this person's position.

**Have you known anyone like that—someone who seems to love having devotions?**

**How do you feel about him or her?**

## 3 Words from the Word

(15-20 minutes)

Examining the Example of Jesus

Have the group turn to Mark 1:35-37 and read it.

Point out that the previous day in Jesus' life had been a full one. He taught in the synagogue (Mark 1:21-22), cast out a demon (vss. 23-28), healed Peter's mother-in-law (vss. 28-31), and then healed and drove out many demons (vss. 32-34). Verse 35 takes place the next morning.

Reread verses 35-37. Then say something along these lines:

**Look at the three types of people again—the Uptight, the Slow-moving, the Confused. Let's say these people see Jesus coming back from His "quiet time." How might they react? What reasons might they give for not following His example?**

Some possible answers:

(The Uptight: "Isn't it hard to keep up the pace of doing this every day? What if I went to all that trouble and didn't have a "quality time" with God?")

(The Slow-moving: "How could He get up so early? Wasn't it wet praying up there in the dew in the morning?")

(The Confused: "What did He do all that time? How long can a person pray without running out of things to say?")

**Spending time alone with God was a regular event on Jesus' schedule. What do you think He got out of it?**

After discussing replies, you may want to point out that some people misinterpret Jesus' rising early to meet with God as a draining experience instead of a strengthening one. It's true that 40 days of fasting (and probably prayer, too) left Jesus hungry (Luke 4:1, 2). But that doesn't mean He was spiritually weak. Perhaps His 40 days of "devotions" equipped Him to face the temptations of the devil.

Have volunteers read II Peter 1:3-9. Ask the group to search for ideas that could help Christians who are Uptight, Slow-moving, or Confused. Help the search with questions like these:

**What does this tell you about building a devotional life?**

**Do we have the materials?**

**What is the process like?**

**What benefits will we receive?**

As needed, supplement answers with the following.

The Uptight: Verses 5-9 talk about how the spiritual life builds "in increasing measure." Spiritual growth is a process. A rich devotional life doesn't happen immediately just because we want it to. Our devotions will grow with our spiritual lives.

The Slow-moving: God promises that we can "participate in the divine nature and escape the corruption in the world caused by evil desires." God will draw us close to Him and help us overcome our evil or even lazy tendencies.

The Confused: God provides the tools we need. "His divine power has given us everything we need for life and godliness through our knowledge of him who called us by his own glory and goodness." Each step for growth becomes apparent to us as we need it.

Point to the house on Resource 2. Say something like this:

**Building a devotional life is like building a house. You start with the foundations and move upward. You don't expect to build a complete house on the first day.**

## 4 Relaxing the Rules

(10-15 minutes)

Listing Myths about the "Right" Way to Have Devotions

**Christians can get uptight, lazy, or confused about devotions because they have rigid, preconceived ideas of what devotions are. These unwritten "rules" aren't wrong or bad, but they don't describe the only "spiritual" way to have devotions.**

**What "rules" have you heard about the "right" way to have devotions?**

As needed, supplement answers by writing the following "rules" on the chalkboard:

1. Devotions should be consistent.
2. Devotions should be done early in the morning.
3. Devotions should last at least 10 minutes.
4. Devotions should make you feel close to God.

**Why have these "rules" become so important?**

**Are they always valid?**

**How can it be harmful to be overconcerned with them?**

Use the following comments as needed.

*Rule 1: Devotions should be consistent.*

**Consistency is helpful, but maybe it's been stressed too much. We may feel so guilty when we miss a few days that we quit. We've been told that sporadic physical exercise doesn't help us, and we assume that's true with devotions, too. It's not; sporadic devotions can help us get started.**

*Rule 2: Devotions should be done early in the morning.*

**This generally accepted guideline is true for some, but not for all. Consider Diane and Doug.**

**Diane tried getting up in the morning for devotions, but it didn't work. She found that the second half hour of her lunch break worked best for her. It meant that she gave up chats with friends after lunch and window shopping, but it was worth it. At first, she only did it two or three days a week. Now she rarely misses a day.**

**Doug's schedule during the week is hectic. "I only pray here and there on weekdays," he says. "On Saturday mornings and Sunday afternoons, I spend about an hour or so reading the Bible and praying. I'm so much more relaxed on weekends and I get a lot out of it. "**

*Rule 3: Devotions should last at least 10 minutes.*

**It may take time to quiet ourselves and focus on God, but artificial time limits don't always help. It's wiser to start short and let our time with God grow. It doesn't have to last the same amount of time every day.**

*Rule 4. Devotions should make us feel close to God.*

**Sometimes they will; other times they won't. As we progress, they may even make us feel grieved or angry. Devotions aren't a "feel good" exercise, but a chance to get to know God. David had various experiences with God. Some Psalms are rich hymns of praise (Psalm 65); others are forlorn cries for help (Psalm 64).**

Ask several people to finish this statement aloud: **If devotions aren't governed by a list of rules, then I . . .**

(Some possible responses: Have a lot of freedom; don't know what to do; have been too hard on myself; can do what works for me, etc.)

(5-10 minutes)

Gauging Our Hunger to Know God Better

Refer group members to Part II of Resource 1. Have them form groups of three or fewer and share their answers to the questions on the sheet.

Then wrap up the discussion:

**If you're frustrated with your devotional life, you're not alone. And you may be surprised to know that your frustration is not a sign of weakness. It's a sign of unfulfilled spiritual desire. You want to know God better than you do now.**

**Richard Foster puts it this way:**

**"Rather than flagellating ourselves for our obvious lack, we should remember that God always meets us where we are and moves us into deeper things."**

If you'd like to prepare the group for next time, pass out copies of Resource 3, "I Knew God Loved Me When . . ." Ask people to complete the sheet this week in preparation for the next session.

Close in prayer, encouraging group members to express silently or audibly their feelings about getting to know God better.

# QUIET TIME QUANDARIES

## PART I

**JEFF . . .**

looks up to Ron, who gets up every morning at 5:00 A.M. and reads his Bible and prays. Jeff has tried this and stopped and started—and stopped. Jeff considers himself a "second-class Christian" and longs to be a "man of God."

**KATHY . . .**

heard a speaker at a women's retreat talk about "quiet times." She tried getting up early, but kept falling asleep.

"It sounded like a good idea," Kathy says, "and everybody says to do it. But I'm just not a morning person. And to be honest, I tried it once and I was bored stiff. I don't seem to be spiritual enough. I don't know if I ever will be."

**DAVE . . .**

hears his pastor talk about having devotions, so he's tried using a devotional book and a read-through-the-Bible-in-a-year program. He prays, but it doesn't seem to "work" for him. These times don't seem to develop his spiritual life as the pastor said they would.

## PART II
## WHICH OF THESE IS TRUE OF YOU?

YES NO 1. I feel a need for spending more time concentrating on God, but I don't really know what the idea of devotions is all about.

YES NO 2. My devotional life frustrates me. I keep hoping it will turn from a discipline to a delight, but so far it hasn't.

YES NO 3. My devotions can be exciting one week and dry the next.

YES NO 4. Devotions are just another legalistic waste of time.

YES NO 5. My devotional life has helped me get beyond the basics into a deeper relationship with God.

# What's Your Type?

## SLOW-MOVING

## CONFUSED

## UPTIGHT

# I Knew God Loved Me When . . .

## DO YOU RECALL A TIME WHEN YOU SENSED THAT GOD LOVED YOU?

**If so, check to indicate the circumstances:**

____ When I barely escaped a tragedy
____ When I received forgiveness that I didn't deserve
____ When I was blessed in an unexpected way
____ When I went to a retreat or prayer service
____ When I thought deeply about Christ's sacrifice on the cross
____ Other ______________________________

**Describe the incident and your feelings. Use these questions to help you. Was anyone else involved? If so, was that person or persons also expressing love to you?**

**Check any of the elements below that were a part of it:**

____ Scripture reading (Do you remember the verses?)
____ Prayer
____ Meditation
____ Writing in a journal or diary
____ Worship

**How did you respond to God?**

____ Thankfulness
____ Forgot to thank Him for a while (Note: This isn't unusual)
____ Made promises to be more obedient
____ Experienced a closer walk with God
____ Expressed joy in some way such as singing
____ Told someone about it
____ Other ______________________________

# HE LOVES ME!

## The Reason for a Devotional Life

If you used Session 1, you urged your group members to eliminate the "rules" of devotions. In this session, you'll help them focus on the *relationship* involved.

"But wait a minute," you may be saying. "I picked this book because it sounded like a how-to course. I want to teach people *how* to develop their devotional lives."

Don't worry. You'll start studying specific activities within the devotional life in the next session. In this session, you'll discuss the foundation for devotions—God's love. Devotions wouldn't be necessary or possible if God didn't love us and want us to know Him. In fact, His love is what makes devotions interesting—and, sometimes, even fun. They help us get to know Someone who has already decided He loves us.

You're about to explore the depths of God's love. You'll let your group members honestly examine how they view God. And you'll show them how God's love can bring wholeness to their lives.

### Where You're Headed:

To help your group members understand God's unconditional love, and how that relates to our devotional "performance."

### Scriptures You'll Apply:

Hosea 1–3; Luke 15:1-24

### Things You'll Need:

- Bibles
- Pens or pencils
- Paper
- Chalkboard and chalk or newsprint and marker
- Resource 4, "Anatomy of a Romance," and Resource 5, "Does God Love You . . . ?" copied as transparencies or handouts
- Overhead projection equipment (optional)
- Copies of Resource 6, "I'm Taking a Survey" (optional)

## 1
# Who Needs Devotions?

(5-10 minutes)

Relating Wants, Needs, and Devotions

Have a couple of volunteers come up to the front of the room. Let them know that they're going to do a little acting for you. Ask each one to think of a situation in which he or she feels content—and act it out in pantomime. Situations might include fishing, working at a hobby, listening to music, etc.

As both pantomime these activities, make comments like the following:

**These people look pretty content. Let's say that they're Christians. They go to church and read the Bible occasionally. They haven't set aside a "quiet time" to spend with God, but they look happy and productive.**

**What could they be missing by not making a special effort for devotions?** (Knowing God and His love more deeply; getting assurance and guidance, etc.)

Thank your actors and let them sit down again. Explain: **We do the things we either *need* to do or *want* to do. A guy who chooses extra snoozing over praying probably doesn't *want* to have devotions. A busy woman *needs* to spend time with her family and get things done—so she skips devotions, too. What makes a person *need* or even *want* to have time alone focusing on God?**

After listening to your group members' ideas, offer an explanation like this:

**We *need* devotions when we realize that no one can meet our needs as God can. The "self" is too fragile an object on which to lean completely. Leaning on our spouses suffocates them. Our work, our friendships, our extended family or even our church fellowship is not strong enough to sustain us.**

**They make fine supplemental supports, but never a core support.**

**We will likely *want* to have devotions as we come to experience, more and more, the genuine love and understanding that God extends to us unconditionally. Here is Someone we can spend time with and not be afraid of being cut down. God's love encourages and stretches us, but it will never reject us, in spite of our weaknesses and failures.**

**Does that explanation ring true to you? Does any part of it sound hard to believe?**

As needed, observe that many people don't really believe that God loves them—or that spending time concentrating on Him will do them much good. Some find it hard to believe that God would want to spend time with them, either.

**Why would God want to hear from us anyway?**

Suggest that group members think of reasons from Scripture or from their own experiences as parents. God is our Father; He delights in our praise and companionship (He walked with Adam in the Garden of Eden); like any parent, He would like to hear from us more frequently than when we just need money!

## 2 Boy Meets Girl

(15-20 minutes)

Looking at a Biblical Example of God's Unconditional Love

Display Resource 4, "Anatomy of a Romance," either as an overhead transparency or a handout. If you use the Resource as a handout, have participants fill it in as you go along.

Ask group members to turn to Hosea 1. This short, seldom-read book tells about a marital relationship with many ups and downs. It pictures our relationship with God. Tell group members that you'll read a passage, explain it, and then ask their opinion about where on the chart you should plot the couple's "success." Here are the passages and information to use in your explanations.

*Hosea 1:2*

God commanded Hosea, a godly man, to marry Gomer, who became a prostitute. (Theologians disagree about whether God wanted Hosea to marry a prostitute or a woman who would become one. One commentator says that the original language points to the translation: "a woman who would lapse into adultery.")

Make a mark high on the chart over "Boy meets girl." Color in a column from zero up to that mark. Since Hosea was a godly man, they had a decent chance. Then make a mark very low over "Girl turns bad," since Gomer committed adultery.

*Hosea 2:4, 5*

Both of these verses (and 1:3, 6, 8) cast doubt on whether Hosea was the father of at least two and perhaps all three of the children. Gomer also wrongly assumed her blessings came from her lovers.

Ask the group to tell you where to make a mark on the graph over "Girl rejects boy" and do so.

*Hosea 2:6, 7, 9*

Hosea built a hedge of thornbushes around Gomer so that she could not find her lovers. Ask people to imagine how embarrassing it would be to see a spouse chasing after his or her lovers. When Gomer refused to acknowledge Hosea as the source of her blessings, Hosea withdrew them (vs. 9).

Ask group for feedback and mark the graph over "Boy tries to woo girl back."

*Hosea 3:1, 2*

Even though Gomer rejected Hosea, God told him to go after her. God comes after us the same way, even when we rebel. Hosea bought Gomer back out of slavery (15 shekels was half the price of a slave), as God bought us back with the price of His Son.

*Hosea 2:14-16*

Hosea was tender with Gomer. He didn't want to be her master, but her husband. He restored her and wanted her to be joyful.

Ask the group to suggest where you should mark the graph over "Girl comes back, boy accepts her." Then read the subtitles below the graph to summarize the story.

**In what ways did Gomer reject Hosea as a husband?** (As a sexual partner and provider.)

**What verses tell us that Hosea still loved and accepted Gomer?** (2:14-16; also see 2:19, 20.)

**How do you think Gomer felt about Hosea's great love for her?** (Perhaps overwhelmed, secure, maybe even guilty.)

**This account illustrates how Israel rejected God (1:2). We're often like Israel—faithful one day and forgetful the next. This account tells us that just as Hosea kept loving Gomer, God continues to love us. He doesn't wait for us to be perfect. "While we were still sinners, Christ died for us." (Romans 5:8).**

(10-15 minutes)

Thinking about Our Personal Views of God

Display or distribute Resource 5, "Does God Love You . . . ?" and look at the cartoons together.

Explain that these pictures represent correct and incorrect views of God that many Christians have. **Which view comes closest to the way you feel yourself relating to God most of the time?**

After people have responded, you may want to comment that just because the loving father of the prodigal son is the correct and biblical image, it doesn't mean that we presently relate to God in this way. Most of us need to develop our sense of God's loving care for us.

**Why don't people accept this image of God?** (They didn't see God's love reflected in their own parents; they have listened to other people's wrong impressions of God; they are put off by Old Testament passages of God destroying nations, etc.)

Point out that these difficulties can be remedied by contemplating or "soaking in" Bible passages that give a balanced view of God's love (such as I John 4:18; 5:3 and Luke 15:3-24, which follow). Concerning the last objection, the Old Testament narratives are sometimes taken out of context. God was actually patient with nations, giving them repeated warnings before destroying them.

Some students might suggest that the courtroom judge is also a correct answer because obedience is important. It's true that God demands our obedience to Christ, but He doesn't want us to fear Him unnecessarily or feel burdened by His commands (see I John 4:18; 5:3).

To illustrate that God is a tough but loving Teacher, you might share the following illustration:

**Imagine that you're a high school student. You come into class and find a list of impossible assignments on the chalkboard. You go home thinking you'll never get your homework done.**

**You sit down to do your homework and someone knocks at the door. It's a tutor (the Holy Spirit) who says, "The teacher sent me to help. The teacher and I will supply what you need to finish the assignments."**

**God loves us and equips us to obey.**

**So why do we obey? To earn God's love?**

Let the group wrestle with the real reasons for obedience. Observe that obedience is an important response to God. It's not a condition for His love. The legalism approach says, "I am worthwhile because I obey." The grace approach says, "I am worthwhile because God loves me."

The legalism approach says, "God loves me because I obey so well." The grace approach says, "God loves me because He decided to love me."

# 4

# Parable Update

(10-15 minutes)

Developing Contemporary Word Pictures of God's Love

**God's love for us is not a simple fact that can be memorized like our telephone numbers. We have to soak in it, as a cucumber soaks for days until it becomes a pickle. It takes time and constant reminding. Word pictures are one way to saturate our minds. Can you think of any familiar parables that are examples of God's love for us?**

As needed, point out these examples:

• *The Diligent Shepherd.* He wasn't satisfied with 99 of the sheep. He went after the other lost one (Luke 15:3-7).

• *The Patient Housekeeper.* She swept the straw-covered floor of the Palestinian hut to find the tenth coin. She had the nine coins, but she wanted to find that tenth one (Luke 15:8-10).

• *The Loving Father.* He didn't grill the prodigal son about his behavior when he returned. The father ran down the road to meet the son. He spared no expense to welcome the boy home (Luke 15:11-24).

Form small groups. Distribute paper and pencils and appoint a recorder for each group.

Ask the groups to brainstorm at least three word pictures of God's love from 20th-century life. They should be amazing examples of people going the extra mile. Here are a few examples:

• A woman who has a baby instead of an abortion, even though it isn't medically safe for her to deliver.

• A paramedic who rushes to save an AIDS patient's life even though it will expose him to the patient's blood and, hence, to the virus; the paramedic then visits the patient every day in the hospital.

Circulate among the small groups to see how they're doing.

After allowing them about five minutes, ask each group to share its best example with the whole group.

Then ask: **How does your sense of God's love for you compare to the kind of love described in your 20th-century example?**

**How could remembering your modern example help you be less "sleepy" when it comes to spending time with God?**

**How could your reminder help you feel less guilty about having a less than perfect quiet time?**

Close the session with prayer for a new sense of God's love to flow into your group members' lives.

If you want to prepare the group for next time, distribute Resource 6. Ask group members to interview at least two people, if possible, before the next session.

# ANATOMY OF A ROMANCE

## Hosea and Gomer's Relationship Status Report

| | | Hosea<br>Boy meets girl | 1:2<br>Girl turns bad | 2:5<br>Girl rejects boy | 2:6, 7, 9<br>Boy tries to woo girl back | 2:14-16<br>Girl comes back; boy accepts her |
|---|---|---|---|---|---|---|
| Successful | 100% | | | | | |
| | 90 | | | | | |
| | 80 | | | | | |
| | 70 | | | | | |
| | 60 | | | | | |
| | 50 | | | | | |
| | 40 | | | | | |
| | 30 | | | | | |
| | 20 | | | | | |
| | 10 | | | | | |
| Unsuccessful | 0 | | | | | |

# Does God Love You . . .

**. . . only if you're good?**

**. . . only when you're busy serving Him?**

**. . . or at least He did at one time?**

**. . . only when it's convenient?**

**. . . only if you obey the law?**

**. . . no matter what?**

# I'M TAKING A SURVEY

**A**sk these questions of two friends, relatives or co-workers (or just answer them yourself if you like). The people you interview need to be somewhat familiar with the Bible, but they don't have to be Christians.

**1.** What's your favorite verse or passage of the Bible?

a.

b.

**2.** When, if ever, do you feel the need to read the Bible?

a.

b.

**3.** What good does Bible reading do?

a.

b.

**4.** Why do you think some people get more out of Bible reading than others do? Is it . . .

Education?

Eagerness?

Openness before God?

Other? (Please specify)

# CONFESSIONS OF A BORED BIBLE READER

## Skills for Devotional Bible Reading

Many of your group members have probably thought to themselves, *I really should read the Bible more.* Don't let them get discouraged by this thought, but encourage them. It shows that they have a spiritual hunger that longs to be satisfied.

Today's session will equip your group members with tools for devotional Bible reading. Some of these tools are simply crucial attitudes that we lack, so this session deals with motivations as well as methods.

A few group members may want to focus on Bible study instead of devotional Bible reading. Though they often overlap, there is a difference. Bible study usually helps people discover what the Bible says in a way that applies to people in general; devotional Bible reading helps them discover what God is saying to them personally through the words of the Bible. Both are important, but today's session will focus on devotional Bible reading.

### Where You're Headed

To equip group members with motivation and tools for devotional Bible study.

### Scriptures You'll Apply

Psalm 119:97-104; Matthew 13:9-15; I Corinthians 2:6-14; Hebrews 4:12

### Things You'll Need

- Bibles
- Pens or pencils
- Paper
- Chalkboard and chalk or other display surface
- Resource 7, "Bible Reading Blues," copied as a transparency or as a handout
- Overhead projection equipment (optional)
- Copies of Resource 8, "Letting God Speak"
- Copies of Resource 9, "Mulling Over Meditation" (optional)

# 1 Word Power

(8-10 minutes)

Thinking about the Bible's Value in a Christian's Life

Distribute paper and pencil to each group member.

**In New Testament times when Roman soldiers dominated life, the Bible was called a double-edged sword. In Old Testament times, the prophet Jeremiah described God's Word as a fire and a hammer (Jeremiah 23:29). In both cases, it was a tool for accomplishing a task.**

Ask group members to list or draw contemporary symbols for the Bible. They should reflect our culture—especially its technological, medical, and communication advances. Here are a few examples to get group members started. The Bible could be compared to:

- Spell-checking computer software (the Bible checks attitudes);
- "Weed and feed" lawn spray that kills weeds and feeds grass (the Bible kills sinful habits and feeds spiritual growth);
- Surgical removal of tumors (the Bible helps us locate our sin and remove it).

Some group members may find it easier to work with a partner or two.

When they've finished, ask them to share their ideas with the group. Then discuss:

**Do you believe the Bible is an effective tool for you today? Why or why not?**

If time allows, ask people to react to the following two quotes on the Bible's relevance today—one on the lighter side, one more serious:

1. **"The Bible contains much that is relevant today, like Noah taking forty days to find a place to park"** (Laurence Peter, *Peter's Quotations*, Bantam Books).

2. **"The Word of God can give joy to help counteract depression. In I John 2:14 the apostle noted that he was writing to young men who were strong and in whom the Word of God was abiding. They were strong emotionally precisely because the Word of God was abiding in them. They had reprogrammed their computer according to the Word of God, and therefore, they were strong and stable emotionally"** (Psychologists Frank Minirth and Paul Meier, *Happiness Is a Choice*, Baker Book House).

# 2 Does the Word Work?

(20-25 minutes)

Looking at Reasons Why Bible Reading May Not Be Meaningful

Display Resource 7, "Bible Reading Blues" (or distribute copies of it as handouts). Give an example of when you've experienced one of these feelings yourself. Then point to each cartoon and ask for a show of hands of those who have uttered a similar complaint. (This will help you determine the most troublesome spots for your group members.)

Form small groups. Assign one of the excuses from Resource 7 to each group (or to individuals, if the whole group is small). Then read the instructions under "Solutions" together. Ask groups to link the principles they find in the "solutions" passages to their assigned "complaint." Circulate among the groups to offer help with understanding the principles in the Scripture. Here are some principles that your group members might find.

*Psalm 119:97-104.* The Bible can be a continuous delight (vss. 97, 103). It gives us understanding and insight (vss. 98-100). It helps us obey God (vss. 101, 102, 104). (Match with excuses 1, 2, 3.)

*Matthew 13:9-15.* Understanding God's Word is a skill that snowballs (vs. 12). The more we seek to understand, the more we will understand. Commitment to God (such as the disciples had) helps us understand Scripture better. The "calloused" (vs. 15) "hardly hear with their ears." If we have callous motives, they may interfere with our hearing. (Match with excuses 1, 3, 4.)

*I Corinthians 2:6-14.* Intellect and emotion are not enough. Spiritual discernment is important, too (vs. 11). (Match with excuses 1-4.)

*Hebrews 4:12.* Scripture is able to penetrate and convict us like nothing else. (Match with excuses 2, 3.)

After group members have finished researching and matching, discuss each complaint. Use the following notes for comments as needed.

*1. I don't get anything out of the Bible. It didn't say anything to me.*

We need to approach the Bible with a spirit of expectancy. Before we read the passage, we think: What may God be saying to me through this book? We release ourselves to God's purposes even before we know what they are. This will help us be receptive and open. When we don't do this, we dull our spiritual senses. Familiar passages especially can fool us. We think we've already absorbed as much from them as possible.

To make this concept more visual, you might draw three descending stair steps on the chalkboard. On the highest step write "No Expectation." On the next lower step write, "No Concentration." On the lowest step write, "No Application." Explain that this is a downward progression.

*2. I'm rushing through this. I'm distracted or in a hurry.*

Hurry is a common roadblock to spiritual sensitivity. We become callous because we have other important tasks to do. Concentration (helped by reading the passage twice if necessary) and preparation (seeking God's blessing before we read) are important.

Share these illustrations if you have time:

**1. Many of the people in Diane and Steve's church are reading the Bible through in a year. "Too often," Steve confesses, "we settle down to watch television and then remember the Bible reading. So we shut off the TV and pull out the Bible. We don't get anything out of it because we haven't prepared ourselves."**

**2. Before reading the Bible, we need to consciously set aside our tasks and problems and quiet our inner selves to listen to God. Here's an example of how John Baillie centered down** (from his book *A Diary of Private Prayer*, Charles Scribner's Sons): **"Almighty God, in this quiet hour I seek communion with thee. From the fret and fever of the day's business, from the world's discordant noises, from the praise and blame of men, from the confused thoughts and vain imaginations of my own heart, I would now turn aside and seek the quietness of thy presence."**

*3. I'm reading the Bible because Christians are supposed to do this.*

The above principles apply, as well as the problem of a "works" attitude. Obeying the "letter of the law," but ignoring the "spirit of the law," seems to block our understanding (II Corinthians 3:6).

*4. I don't understand what this passage is saying.*

The Bible is practical beyond what we can imagine. The psalmist even describes the Bible as "honey" and "gold" (Psalm 119:103, 127).

Sometimes we don't understand a verse even after we tune into it with spiritual senses and study it carefully. It's a good idea to make a note of it in a journal so you can come back to it later. Perhaps we won't understand it until we've grown in our spiritual walk or even until we've arrived in heaven.

When a Bible verse or passage puzzles you:

- Read the verses (or chapters) before and after it.
- Read similar verses and parallel passages suggested in the margins.
- Read reference material at the beginning of the Bible book. Outlines and historical and biographical information often shed light.
- Ask for help from a "resource friend," such as a Bible teacher who enjoys answering your questions.

To wrap up this step, share the following quotes if you have time:

**"Everything depends on how we read [the Bible] . . on how we smuggle ourselves into its words, and allow the texture of a text to weave its web around us"** (Michael Fishbane, *Text and Texture*, Schocken Books).

**"What you bring away from the Bible depends to some extent on what you carry to it"** (Oliver Wendell Holmes, Sr.)

(12-15 minutes)

Rehearsing a Devotional Bible Reading Session

**Maybe you're more used to Bible study than to devotional Bible reading. How are the two different?**

As needed, share these ideas:

Bible study tends to ask in a general, objective way, "What does this passage say? What is its significance?" It analyzes meanings of words; notes context in history; uses a word-for-word Bible translation; and uses study tools such as Bible dictionaries and concordances.

Devotional Bible reading, on the other hand, tends to focus on the personal significance of the passage. It may involve a variety of Bible translations and paraphrases and devotional books. It speaks to the reader's personal spiritual growth and must be more than an intellectual exercise.

**So let's try some devotional Bible reading.**

Give a copy of Resource 8, "Letting God Speak," to each person. Distribute Bibles as needed. Ask group members to scatter their seating throughout the room if possible.

**I'll give step-by-step directions to lead you through your own private devotional Bible reading time. After each instruction, I'll allow you time to follow that instruction. If I interrupt you in a**

**previous step, make note of what I've said, complete that step, and then continue.**

Use steps similar to these:

**1. Pray a prayer of expectancy: What may God be saying to me through this book?**

(Allow 1 minute of silence.)

**2. Turn to James 1:1-8 and read it. Then read it again and concentrate on it.**

(Allow 5 minutes.)

**3. Examine what you've read, using the questions on the top portion of Resource 8. Pick the questions that have the most relevance to this passage and skip the others.**

(Allow 6-8 minutes.)

**4. Close with a short prayer, expressing to the Lord your feelings about what you've read and thought here. Ask Him to help you sense His presence during the rest of the day.**

(Allow 1 minute of silence.)

Encourage group members to continue reading through the Book of James this week, using the questions on Resource 8.

If you'd like to prepare the group for next time, distribute copies of Resource 9, "Mulling over Meditation." Ask group members to mark their responses to the quotations before the next session.

## 4 Quiet-Timely Tips (optional)

(5-12 minutes)

Listing Devotional Bible Reading Methods

If you have time, discuss some or all of the following ideas for devotional Bible reading.

*Systems*

Ask the group to help you list systems for devotional Bible reading that they've used or heard about. To help them get started, you may want to share ideas from this list:

- A chapter of Proverbs a day. (Read the chapter that corresponds to the day's date.)
- Five psalms a day. (Read the chapter that corresponds to the date multiplied by five, plus the four psalms before it.)
- The Gospels in a month. (Divide the number of pages for the Gospel by the number of days in the month and read that many pages a day.)

*Topics*

The following ideas are examples of "point of need" devotionals. They create a high expectancy level because readers know what they're searching for.

- A Gospel, noting how Jesus met people's needs.
- Philippians, looking for verses on contentment.
- Old Testament character studies that apply to our struggles. (Are you a "grasper" like Jacob? Read about this tricky man's encounters with God in Genesis 27–35.)
- Proverbs, noting verses about a topic such as money, friendship, wisdom, or speech.
- Categorizing psalms according to praise, thankfulness, and requests for help.

• Topical searches (using a concordance) on forgiveness, love, meekness, anger, heaven, etc.

*Methods*

• When you read, it helps to limit yourself to five or six verses of teaching passages (such as the New Testament epistles), or one episode in narrative passages (such as the Gospels or Old Testament stories), or a single psalm, or a few proverbs.

• When you study narrative passages, ask yourself: "If I had been there, how would I have felt? In what ways am I like or unlike this Bible person?"

• Keep in mind that devotional books have advantages and disadvantages. They can make a passage clearer and easier to apply. Sometimes, however, we risk substituting them for prayer and Scripture reading itself.

• It's good to have goals in Bible reading—unless it makes you feel hurried or overwhelmed. For devotional Bible reading, it's important to read slowly. When a passage touches you, savor it and meditate on it.

# BIBLE READING BLUES

# COMPLAINTS

**1.** I don't get anything out of the Bible. It doesn't say anything to me.
**2.** I'm rushing through this. I'm distracted or in a hurry.
**3.** I'm doing this because Christians are supposed to do this.
**4.** I don't understand what this passage is saying.

# SOLUTIONS

What does each of these passages below say to the above complaints we have about Bible reading? What do these passages imply about how we should approach Bible reading?
As you read these verses, write portions of them next to the excuses they answer.

**a.** Psalm 119:97-104

**b.** Matthew 13:9-15

**c.** I Corinthians 2:6-14

**d.** Hebrews 4:12

# Letting God Speak

## Ask: What does this passage say about . . .

- Good and bad attitudes and their results?
- Release from fear, hate, and other negative feelings?
- How I should act—changes I should make, actions to correct?
- Sins that I need to forsake and confess?
- How the persons mentioned are examples for me; how I can be more like them?
- Challenges that I should take up with my job, family, friends, church; first steps in taking up these challenges?
- Promises I can claim; conditions I need to meet?

| When you need . . . | Read . . . |
|---|---|
| • comfort | Isaiah 43:1-7; II Corinthians 1:3-7 |
| • strength | Isaiah 40:28-31; John 14:1-3, 12-21 |
| • courage | II Timothy 1:3-12 |
| • to overcome temptation | I Corinthians 10:1-13 |
| • to understand or show love | I Corinthians 13:1-13 |
| • joy and contentment | Philippians 4:4-9 |
| • guidance for taming the tongue | James 3:1-12; Matthew 12:33-37 |
| • help with life's purpose | Galatians 2:20 |
| • to pray for others | Colossians 1:9-14; Philippians 1:9-11 |
| • to look forward to the Second Coming | I Corinthians 15:51-58<br>I Thessalonians 5:1-11 |
| • to praise God | Psalms 92–100 |
| • to form spiritual goals | Matthew 5:3-12 |
| • to overcome preoccupation with money | Matthew 6:19-21, 25-34 |
| • to stop criticizing others | Matthew 7:1-5 |

# Mulling over Meditation

**Read the thoughts below about meditation and then use one of these marks to show your response to each.**

I have a question about this.

I understand this.

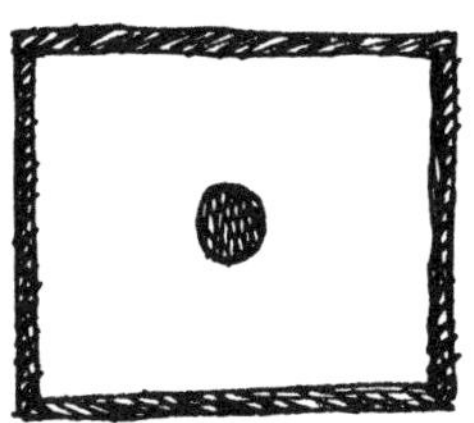

I'm especially interested in this.

I disagree with this.

☐ Meditation is often compared to chewing food because the word *ruminate* means "to chew the cud" or "to meditate at length" (*American Heritage Dictionary*). When dental problems prevent us from chewing our food, we eventually have digestive and intestinal problems. Perhaps we suffer from "spiritual indigestion" because we hear God's word taught, but we don't digest it in meditation.

*Jan Johnson*

☐ Eastern forms of meditation stress the need to become detached from the world, to lose our individuality and merge with the Cosmic Mind. Christian meditation is detachment from the confusion of this world and attachment to God. The first is an emptying only; the second is an emptying and then a refilling with God.

*adapted from Richard Foster,*
Celebration of Discipline, *Harper and Row Publishers*

☐ "Reflection and meditation demand a certain amount of imagination. . . . When we read the passages describing Jesus' ministry, our reflecting minds place ourselves right into the story: we see the Savior heal, hear Him teach, and respond to His directives."

*Gordon MacDonald,* Ordering Your Private World, *Oliver Nelson*

☐ "In meditation we latch onto phrases from the prophets, memorizing small portions, and we allow the words to trickle down over the structures of our inner being as we repeat them over and over again. From such exercises come new and wonderful conclusions."

*Gordon MacDonald,* Ordering Your Private World

# SOAKING IN THE SCRIPTURE

## Meditating on God's Word

Most Christians have a vague idea of what meditation is, but feel uncomfortable with it. For some it smacks of New Age or Eastern mysticism. But as Richard Foster explains in his book *Celebration of Discipline* (Harper and Row Publishers), Eastern forms of meditation stress the need to become detached from the world, to lose our individuality and merge with the "Cosmic Mind." Christian meditation is detachment from the confusion of this world and attachment to God. The first is an emptying only; the second is an emptying and then a refilling with God.

Other Christians look askance at meditation because it doesn't seem as concrete as reading the Bible or praying. We know what these behaviors look like, but a person who's meditating looks as if he or she is falling asleep!

Christians meditate much more than they realize. We chew on Scripture by going over what we've read. This thoughtful application of Scripture is one of the most familiar forms of meditation.

Meditation expands the previous session's theme of taking in the Scripture. In that session we discovered and applied key ideas and incidents from Scripture. In this session, we'll "chew" on them.

### Where You're Headed

To help participants understand the mechanics and motivation of meditation.

### Scriptures You'll Apply

Psalm 1:1-3; 48:9; 77:12; 104:34; 119:48, 148; 143:5; 145:5

### Things You'll Need

- Bibles
- Pens or pencils
- Paper
- Chalkboard and chalk or other display surface
- Copies of Resource 9, "Mulling over Meditation," for those who don't have them from last week
- Resource 10, "Meditate? How?" copied as a transparency or a handout
- Overhead projection equipment (optional)
- Copies of Resource 11, "Meditation Situations"
- Copies of Resource 12, "Prayerstyles of the Rather Famous" (optional)

# 1 Meditation Muddle

(10-12 minutes)

Creating Interest in Meditation

Distribute pencils and copies of Resource 9, "Mulling over Meditation," from the previous session. Ask any who brought their sheets back from last time to look at them.

Read the instructions and the first quote together. Then ask people to mark the quote accordingly. Do the same with each quote.

After you've finished, ask volunteers to tell which quotes they marked with an exclamation mark or the "X." You may want to highlight material related to these as the session continues.

Ask what questions people have about any of the quotes. If their questions will be answered later, explain this and don't take time with them now. If you don't think their questions will be addressed, you can offer an explanation now or write the questions down for further study.

Optional opener: Before the session, write these four categories on the chalkboard or other display surface:

TOTAL CONFUSION: What in the world is Christian meditation?

DISTANT CONFUSION: I've heard about meditation, but never tried it.

CLOSE-UP CONFUSION: I tried meditating, but was confused.

CLOSE-UP INTERACTION: I tried meditating and got something out of it.

Display the categories now. Ask group members to decide into which of these categories they belong. Then read the first one and ask group members who fall in this category to raise their hands. Do the same with the other three. Ask those who put themselves in the last category to share one of their experiences.

**If you're confused about meditation, it's no wonder. Our society is skeptical about anything that looks like inactivity. As Ralph Waldo Emerson said in 1833, "If a man sits down to think, he is immediately asked if he has a headache."**

# 2 Meditation Master Plan

(20-25 minutes)

Looking at What the Bible Says about Meditation

Display Resource 10, "Meditate? How?" as a transparency, or distribute photocopies of it as handouts. First, read the two questions. Then ask a volunteer to read each passage and answer the questions. Not all passages answer both questions. Here are some answers group members might find.

*Psalm 1:1-3*

Question 1: (The person who meditates doesn't have wicked cohorts [vs. 1]; he delights in the law of the Lord [vs. 2]. He is as stable as a tree planted by the water and as prosperous as a fruit tree in season [vs. 3].)

Question 2: (The law of the Lord [implied from vs. 2].)

*Psalm 48:9*

Question 2: (God's unfailing love. God's unfailing kindness and love are mentioned over and over in Scripture. [You may recognize "unfailing" as "steadfast" if you use the *King James Version*].)

*Psalm 77:12*

Question 2: (All of God's works and His mighty deeds. These

apply to God's work in the past through Israel and the church and today in our lives.)

*Psalm 104:34*

Question 1: (Meditation isn't so serious that it's joyless. The Psalm writer rejoiced in the Lord as he meditated on Him. He also wanted his meditation to please God.)

*Psalm 119:48*

Question 2: (God's decrees [commands and statutes].)

*Psalm 119:148*

Question 1: (When the meditator can't sleep, he prays. Perhaps he even chooses to meditate rather than sleep.)

Question 2: (God's promises.)

*Psalm 143:5*

Question 2: (This psalmist meditates on the past, recalling God's works, the things His hands have done. This could refer to past deeds or even creation.)

*Psalm 145:5*

Question 2: (God's wonderful works. Surrounding phrases speak of the glorious splendor of God's majesty and the power of God's awesome works.)

Summarize by writing these four major topics for meditation on the bottom of the transparency or on the board:

- God's unfailing love
- God's wonderful works
- God's commandments
- God's promises.

If time allows, you might share the following examples of passages in all four categories for later meditation.

*Examples of God's unfailing love:*

- Jesus loved Peter even after he denied Him (John 21:15)
- God loves us even though we're sinners (Romans 5:8)

*Examples of God's wonderful works:*

- God delivered Israel (Psalm 106:8)
- God sits enthroned in heaven (Isaiah 40:22)

*Examples of God's commandments:*

- To be honest (Colossians 3:9)
- To be sexually pure (I Corinthians 6:18)

*Examples of God's promises:*

- Eternal life to those who believe (Romans 6:8)
- Christ's return (II Peter 3:9)

## 3

## Meditation Situations

(10-12 minutes)

Looking at Models of Meditation

Distribute Resource 11, "Meditation Situations," to each participant and read each anecdote.

Then have the group break into teams of three or fewer and discuss the questions at the bottom of the sheet.

After discussion, say something like this: **If you've had any positive experiences with meditating on Scripture, tell us what has worked for you.**

As needed, supplement replies with tips like the following:

- Choose a place that is quiet and free from such interruptions as the telephone. A designated spot may help.

• Use a posture that is not tense nor too relaxed. You want to be quiet, but alert.

• Reflect on a single event, parable, a few verses, even a word that holds special meaning. Use your senses: See the storms, feel the sea spray on your back.

• Begin with a time of "centering down," or quieting yourself. Turn each of your earthly thoughts and concerns over to God one by one. Then come back to Scripture.

—ideas from *Celebration of Discipline* by Richard Foster, Harper and Row Publishers.

• "It has proved useful to meditate for a whole week on a text of approximately 10 to 15 verses. It is not good to meditate on a different text each day, as our receptiveness is not always the same and the texts are usually far too long"—Dietrich Bonhoeffer.

## 4 Meditation Audition

(5-10 minutes)

Trying a Time of Focused Meditation

Distribute Bibles as needed. Suggest that group members position themselves as far apart from each other as possible in your meeting area. Ask them to choose one of the Psalms passages from Resource 10, reread it, and then meditate on it.

Allow 3-5 minutes for meditation. Then close in prayer. If you have time, ask your group members to share their reactions.

If you'd like to prepare people for next time, pass out copies of Resource 12, "Prayerstyles of the Rather Famous." Ask group members to take the quiz this week.

# MEDITATE? HOW?

**Psalm 1:1-3** **Psalm 77:12** **Psalm 119:48, 148**

**Psalm 48:9** **Psalm 104:34** **Psalm 143:5**

**Psalm 145:5**

**1.** What is it like to meditate? What are the benefits?

**2.** On what exactly did the psalmist meditate?

# MEDITATION SITUATIONS

## CASUAL MEDITATION

• Chuck is experimenting with concentrating on Scripture. He wondered, *Could I use my commuting time to meditate?* He decided he could if it was a casual, "memorizing in your sleep" method. So he borrowed some cassette tapes of Scripture. He plays one for five minutes. Then he "stews" on what he hears.

• Laurie cares for two lively preschool children all day, but she's interested in "meditating on the run." So she snatches time early in the day for a short devotional Bible reading. Then she leaves her Bible lying on the dining room table open to that day's passage. As she whizzes by it during the day, she peeks at the Scripture so that she can keep pondering it as she changes diapers and feeds her children.

## FOCUSED MEDITATION

• Denise slips into an old church near her work in the downtown area for a few minutes on her lunch hour. She brings her Bible and turns to a different psalm each day. She reads it until a verse jumps out at her; then she closes her eyes and concentrates on what it says.

• Every few days, Bill sets aside a short time of quiet. He sits in front of a window that looks out on trees. He says this short prayer: "Lord, show me something of Yourself today." Then he reads an episode from the Gospels and imagines himself in the story. Usually he's an onlooker who's amazed at Jesus' behavior. Other times, he's a central character and he finds himself thrilled that Jesus healed him or upset that Jesus rebuked him. Always, Bill looks for ways in which this applies to his life.

• ***What benefits are these people receiving?***

• ***How practical are these methods? Do you have any suggestions or refinements?***

• ***Do any of the situations sound like something you'd like to try? Why or why not?***

# Prayerstyles of the Rather Famous

1. **Who** risked his life rather than give up his daily time of prayer?
2. **Who** got up early in the morning and went to the mountains to pray?
3. **Who** offered prayers of praise, thanks, and requests underwater?
4. **Who** "wrestled in prayer" for the Colossians?
5. **Who** prayed so fervently that the priest thought she was drunk?
6. **Who** spent the night praying to God?
7. **Who** saw the angel Gabriel in the midst of his prayer?
8. **Who** interrupted his private prayers to ask his friends a question?
9. **Who** prayed after talking with the ruler of the land?
10. **Who** prayed while talking with the ruler of the land?

*See answers below.*

1. Daniel (Daniel 6:10) 2. Jesus (Mark 1:35) 3. Jonah (Jonah 2:1-9) 4. Epaphras (Colossians 4:12) 5. Hannah (I Samuel 1:12-14) 6. Jesus (Luke 6:12) 7. Daniel (Daniel 9:21) 8. Jesus (Luke 9:18) 9. Moses (Exodus 8:30; 10:18) 10. Nehemiah (Nehemiah 2:4)

# TALKING WITH ONE WHO LIKES YOU

## Honest, Balanced Prayer

If you're skeptical about covering the subject of prayer in one session, you're smart. Instead of looking at all aspects of prayer, you'll focus sharply on prayer within the devotional time. You'll emphasize a balance among praise, confession, thanks, and intercessory prayer, too.

Devotional prayer times are different from what some call "flash prayers" or "arrow prayers." These quick prayers we offer God throughout the day are filled mostly with requests. Devotional prayer nurtures us and helps us maintain a healthy relationship with God. You'll want to explain this to your group members early in the session to help them stay on track.

### Where You're Headed

To motivate group members to shape their devotional prayer lives with balance and honesty.

### Scriptures You'll Apply

Psalms 33; 51; 86; 116

### Things You'll Need

- Bibles
- Pens or pencils
- Paper
- Chalkboard and chalk or other display surface
- Copies of Resource 13, "P.A.R.T. Praying"
- Resource 14, "Dishonest to God," copied as a transparency or as a handout
- Overhead projection equipment (optional)
- Copies of Resource 15, "Express Yourself" (optional)

## 1
## Have You Got a Prayer?
(7-10 minutes)

Reflecting on Our Feelings about Prayer

Write these descriptions on the chalkboard or other display surface:

- Falling asleep in front of the television
- Talking with a friend on the telephone
- Visiting a therapist
- Getting a performance review from your boss
- Brushing your teeth and other necessary rituals.

Ask people to choose partners and to talk with those partners about which of the activities on the list are most like the way they see devotional prayer. Allow two or three minutes for this.

Then regather as a whole group and continue:

**According to a recent Gallup poll, 3 in 10 of the "unchurched" say religion is very important in their lives; 77 percent say they occasionally pray. Why do you think so many people seem more interested in prayer than in church or "religion"?**

**Do you think most Christians are more interested in praying than in attending church? Why or why not?**

**Do you identify with the man who said the following?**

**"I watch as I fill up every available slot in my appointment book, fill every minute of the day, and do not leave time or space to come wholly into the presence of God with my entire being, my entire self. This is no accident, although I like to pretend that it is. I like to believe that I'm very busy doing God's work, and God, being omniscient, ought to know this and be content to wait until I'm ready to meet—and it looks right now, according to my calendar, as though this meeting might take place sometime in the middle of spring quarter!"** (A pastor, quoted in *Weavings,* March/April 1989)

## 2
## Beyond the Gimme
(25-30 minutes)

Looking at Biblical Examples of Devotional Praying

**Prayer in the devotional life is more balanced than simple "gimme prayers." One easy way to remember at least four components of devotional prayer is this acrostic for the word "PART": Praise, Admit, Request, and Thank.**

**At times these categories are artificial. We can slip easily from one to the other in the same sentence. But they help us organize our prayer time and keep it balanced.**

Distribute Resource 13, "P.A.R.T. Praying," to group members. Form four or more teams (or have people work individually if the group is small). Assign one of the four sections on the sheet to each team or person.

Teams or individuals should search out verses that illustrate the ideas listed. After about ten minutes, ask them to share their answers. Here are some suggestions:

*Praise (Psalm 33)*

- God's good qualities—righteousness, justice, unfailing love (vs. 5)
- God's majesty—God's place in heaven (vss. 13-19)
- God's mighty deeds—works of creation (vss. 6-11)
- The psalmist's responses—singing, playing harp and lyre,

shouting for joy, waiting in hope, rejoicing (vss. 1-3, 20, 21)

*Admit (Psalm 51)*

• Confessing sin—David didn't describe his sin specifically, but the introductory comment says that this was written after he sinned with Bathsheba (II Samuel 11–12) (vss. 3-5)

• Asking forgiveness—he asks for mercy, cleansing, and restoration (vss. 1, 2, 6-12)

• A sense of accountability—he will use his sin to help others; he offers a broken spirit and contrite heart (vss. 13-19, especially vs. 17)

*Request (Psalm 86)*

• Specific requests—the psalmist asks for protection, mercy, joy, strength (vss. 1-4, 6, 7, 14, 16)

• Exploring what the psalmist's part is in getting the prayer answered—this psalmist committed himself to walking in God's truth with an undivided heart, fearing God's name, to praising God and acknowledging His love (vss. 11-13)

• Expressing faith that God will answer—he was confident of God's goodness and abilities and His willingness to answer (vss. 5-10, 15)

*Thank (Psalm 116)*

• The psalmist's problem and how God solved it—the psalmist cried for mercy, was entangled by cords of death; God heard his cry and delivered him (vss. 1-4, 8, 9)

• The psalmist's expression of joyful gratitude—he talked about God's good qualities and deeds, how he wanted to repay the Lord and offer thank offerings (vss. 5, 6, vss. 12-19).

Ask: **Why list praise and thanks separately? Aren't they the same thing?**

As needed, observe that thankfulness can be described as being grateful for what God has done for us. Praise, on the other hand, is recognizing who God is apart from our needs.

## 3 Devotional Detours

(15-20 minutes)

Discussing Three Problems of Devotional Prayer

Use the following comments as needed to summarize three major problems of devotional prayer.

*Problem One: A Lack of Balance*

**Our prayer lives can become lopsided when they exclude activities such as praising, admitting, requesting, and thanking. What's missing in the prayer life of the person who:**

**Never praises?** (Recognizing God's power and majesty.)

**Never admits?** (Recognizing one's own vulnerability.)

**Never requests?** (Trusting God with concerns.)

**Never thanks**? (Recognizing God's past blessings.)

Draw the following scales on the chalkboard or other display surface.

**Where on each of these scales would you place yourself?**

Praises only ———————————— Never praises

Admits only ———————————— Never admits

Requests only ———————————— Never requests

Thanks only ———————————— Never thanks

*Problem Two: A Lack of Honesty*

Display or distribute Resource 14, "Dishonest to God." If you're using it as a transparency, cover the lower portion. If you're using it as a handout, you might want to cut it in half and distribute only the upper portion at this point.

Note that the man in the cartoon has plenty of problems—but he doesn't bring any of them to the Lord.

Read the prayer in the caption and ask these questions:

**What are some other typical rote (memorized, mechanical, or automatic) phrases that Christians use in prayer?**

**How can these rote prayers become spiritual masks?**

**Why are we afraid to be honest with God?**

Uncover the lower portion of Resource 14 and read the question. Wait for people to choose phrases from the list. Give them a chance to share their choices, but avoid pressing them to answer aloud.

*Problem three: A lack of spiritual feeling*

**From our human point of view, we may feel dissatisfied with prayer because we don't feel as if our prayers are answered or that we're getting through to God.**

Ask group members to offer suggestions to help with this.

Then supplement their suggestions with comments like these:

**Emotional highs and spiritual growth aren't the same thing. Prayer is an adventure. We don't pray because "it works." We pray because we love God and want to commune with Him. Sometimes prayer will evoke great spiritual feeling; other times it will leave us with questions that God will keep percolating in us; still other times it won't provide answers, but a willingness (grace, actually) to live without answers. In time, we learn to seek God, the Blesser, not just His blessings. We love Him, not just feelings of being close to Him.**

## 4 Prayer Practice

(5-7 minutes)

Trying New Formats for Praying

Explain that you want group members to have a time of prayer before they leave. Refer to Resource 13 again and encourage them to use a different format than they've ever used before. They might try:

- Focusing on one of the "P.A.R.T." categories they've neglected.
- Moving through all four kinds of prayer.
- Praying a psalm.

Explain that they have only 3-5 minutes to do this.

You might offer the following hints to those who choose to pray a psalm:

1. Change the wording so that you're speaking directly to God. Some psalms are phrased that way. Others have to be altered slightly.
2. Insert your name in appropriate places if you like.
3. Insert your own requests or reasons you're thankful or sins you wish to confess.
4. Let the Book of Psalms be your tutor in prayer.

After group members are finished, close in prayer by thanking

God for new insights about prayer.

If you'd like to prepare people for next time, distribute copies of Resource 15, "Express Yourself." Encourage group members to take the sheet home and figure out which example on the sheet is closest to the way they would like to relate to God.

## 5 Prayer Walk (optional)

(30-60 minutes)

Acting Out the P.A.R.T. Prayer

Here's an idea for an optional event outside your meeting time.

To help make the P.A.R.T. prayer categories more visual, and to give the group added practice in prayer, try a "prayer walk."

Choose a method of transportation your group likes—jogging, walking, bicycling, or driving cars. Map a route around your area and pray together at each spot the kind of prayer appropriate for that spot. Here are some suggestions for stops on your route.

*Praise stop:* a fountain, a creek bed—any place with a view of nature.

*Admit stop:* the parking lot of an "adult" bookstore, or a department store that encourages conspicuous consumption of luxury items.

*Request stop:* the parking lot of a hospital, a street mission, a social security office, or a civic building with a jail in it.

*Thanks stop:* near a bank, a furniture store, a restaurant—any place that sells things your group members are thankful for.

If you make your last stop a restaurant, you might close with a bite to eat there.

# P.A.R.T. Praying

**As** a group, look for your topic in the assigned psalm. Be ready to share this with the whole group. Make notes on the back if you like.

## PRAISE

Psalm 33

**Look in this psalm for:**

• God's good qualities
• God's majesty
• God's mighty deeds
• the psalmist's responses (singing, exalting)

## ADMIT

Psalm 51

**Look in this psalm for:**

• confessing sin
• asking forgiveness
• a sense of accountability and how psalmist wants to change

## REQUEST

Psalm 86

**Look in this psalm for:**

• specific requests
• exploring what the psalmist's part is in getting the prayer answered
• expressing faith that God will answer

## THANK

Psalm 116

**Look in this psalm for:**

• the psalmist's problem and how he solved it
• the psalmist's expression of joyful gratitude

# DISHONEST TO GOD

**"Dear God, thank You for this beautiful day and for the many blessings You have bestowed upon me . . . Oh, yeah, I almost forgot. I need a job—and a life."**

## Which phrase(s) below expresses a new degree of honesty that you would like to add to your prayer life?

### PRAYER IS WHERE I CAN . . .

- be completely myself
- see myself as I really am
- enjoy what God has given me
- argue with God about what's going on
- acknowledge mistakes and set them aside
- learn to love God
- learn to love others as being made in the image of God
- be shaped at my very deepest level

*(adapted from "The Paradox of Prayer," by Robert C. Bondi,* Weavings, *March/April 89)*

# EXPRESS YOURSELF

**Explore the ways you express yourself to God this week. Consider these examples.**

• When **Rosalie** can't pray, she can write. Sometimes she is so angry that she scribbles her prayers in her journal. She finds a release there as in no other way.

• **Dave** is a "doodling journaler." As he thinks, he doodles pictures and thoughts such as: "Where am I going in life?" or "Show me what's happening, Lord."

• **Susan** loves to bake bread. There's something earthy about kneading the dough. On days when Susan feels upset, kneading dough is almost like a prayer. She knows God can see her doing this, and trusts that He understands the feelings she can't put into words.

• **Steve** relates to God best when he's lying on the floor and wearing the headphones to his stereo. He has found some Christian music that expresses the thoughts and desires he wants to express to God, yet seems so incapable of doing with words alone.

• When **Barbara's** family goes camping, she takes her sketch pad along. With pencil (or watercolors if she has time), she records the beauty she sees in the hills and mountains around her. After she's done, she often sits quietly and reflects on the God who has created such wonders.

Can you think of other ways in which people express themselves to God?

# OPENING UP TO GOD

## Expressing Your Thoughts in Journals and Otherwise

More Christians seem to be talking and writing about journaling today than in past years. What is journaling, and what good is it?

Journaling is simply writing down our thoughts about and prayers to God. When we combine it with prayer and Bible study, journaling becomes an outward form of meditation.

Through journaling, we "ruminate" on paper about what God is saying to us in the Bible, and through our victories and failures. Journaling can be especially useful when we're confused about what God is doing in our lives. We "hash it out" on paper as David did in the Psalms. We ask our questions, make some guesses, express our faith.

Journaling is different from prayer because the physical act of writing seems to help us work through our thoughts. That's why the activities in last session's take-home Resource 15 work, too. Woodworking or kneading bread dough can become times of expressing ourselves to God in outward, physical ways.

### Where You're Headed

To help group members understand the purpose and process of journaling and related activities as helps to spiritual growth.

### Scripture You'll Apply

Psalm 56

### Things You'll Need

- Bibles
- Pens or pencils
- Blank lined paper
- Chalkboard and chalk or other display surface
- Resource 16, "Why Bother to Journal?" copied as a transparency or as a handout
- Overhead projection equipment (optional)
- Copies of Resource 17, "Let's Try Journaling"
- Copies of Resource 18, "The Case of the Disappearing Majesty"

# 1
## You Don't Have to Be a Writer
(8-10 minutes)

Getting Rid of Misconceptions about Journaling

Announce that you're going to give the group a quiz. On the first two questions, ask group members to raise their hands when they hear the right answer.

**1. Journaling is . . .**

**(a) Delivering the *Wall Street Journal***

**(b) Subscribing to *Ladies' Home Journal***

**(c) A cruel and unusual form of punishment**

**(d) Writing down everything that happens to you**

**(e) Writing down our thoughts about and prayers to God.**

(The answer, of course, is [e].)

**2. When I first said the word "journaling," which of the following did you feel?**

**(a) Nervous**

**(b) Indifferent**

**(c) Puzzled**

**(d) Hesitant**

**(e) Interested**

**3. I'm going to read five statements. One of them is false. Wait until I've read all five and then tell me which one isn't true.**

**(a) Journaling for spiritual purposes is between you and God only.**

**(b) Punctuation and spelling are important in journaling.**

**(c) A journal is a place in which you can reveal your true feelings.**

**(d) A journal entry can be any length. A long entry isn't necessarily better.**

**(e) A journal doesn't have to be "kept up" every day or every week to be important. Expect lapses of time.**

(Only the second statement is false.)

**When people talk about journaling, does it sound a little scary or boring? You don't have to let the idea of "writing" do that to you.**

**This is nothing like writing high school term papers. You don't have to be Ernest Hemingway or Erma Bombeck. Whatever way you write is your style, and that's enough for journaling. Spelling and grammar aren't important. And for those who can't imagine doing any kind of writing, we'll be talking later about other forms of expression to and about God.**

# 2
## David's Diaries
(25-30 minutes)

Looking at a Biblical "Journal" and Its Purposes

**David was one of the greatest journalers of all time. His "journals" have come down to us as Psalms. For example, David fled for his life from Israel's own king, Saul. David became so desperate that he went to live with an enemy king of Gath. (If you like, read this background from I Samuel 21:10-15.) The inscription of Psalm 56 tells us that David wrote this psalm during these experiences. Let's look first at what David included in his journal.**

Write the following categories on the chalkboard or other display surface. Then read two or three verses at a time from Psalm 56, asking group members to tell into which of the categories that section fits. Suggested answers are in parentheses, but they are not the only possible answers.

- What happened (56:1, 2, 5, 6).
- How he felt about it (56:3, 4, 10, 11)
- What he wanted God to do about the situation (56:7-9)
- What he planned to do about it (56:12, 13)

**How might this journaling process have helped David?**

After people share their ideas, display or pass out Resource 16, "Why Bother to Journal?" Explain each point, using related quotes as needed.

**1.** ***Turn confusion into clarity.***

**Journaling clears our minds. We think about what we want to say and we realize what our true thoughts and feelings are.**

**"Each of us carries on inner conversations as we sort through our feelings about daily living, our relationships, world events. Journaling is the process of writing down those 'talks with ourselves' so that what our mind is thinking and our heart is feeling becomes tangible: ink on paper"** (Anne Broyles in Journaling, *The Upper Room*).

**2.** ***Think "out loud."***

**Here's a sample from Gordon MacDonald's journal** (*Ordering Your Private World,* Oliver Nelson):

**"Lord, what do I really know about drawing upon your strength? I, with the shallow mind, the weak spirit, the minimal discipline. What is there of me that you could use? I have talents, but others have more and use them better. I have experience, but others have greater and have profited deeper. So what is there?**

**"Perhaps the answer lies somewhere in [Hudson] Taylor's comment 'God uses men who are weak and feeble enough to lean on him.' But, Lord, I worry that while I may be weak enough, will I be smart enough to know from whence comes my help?"**

**3.** *Reveal our true selves.*

**A journal is a place to honestly express our true feelings. We find a deeper sense of being accepted by God as we work things out and admit our faults.**

**"A help to me in working things out has been to keep an honest . . . unpublishable journal. . . . If I can write things out I can see them, and they are not trapped within my own subjectivity. I have been keeping these notebooks of thoughts and questions and sometimes just garbage (which needs to be dumped somewhere) since I was about nine, and they are, I think, my free psychiatrist's couch.**

**Not long ago someone I love said something which wounded me grievously, and I was desolate that this person could possibly have made such a comment to me.**

**So, in great pain, I crawled to my journal and wrote it all out in a great burst of self-pity. And when I had set it down, when I had it before me, I saw that something I myself had said had called forth the words which had hurt me so. It had, in fact, been my own fault. But I would never have seen it if I had not**

**written it out"** (Madeleine L'Engle, *Walking on Water*, Harold Shaw Publishers).

4. ***Listen to God.***

**As we write down Scripture and what we know to be God's will despite our feelings, we sense God speaking to us and directing us.**

**"All of this is part of listening to God. As I write, I am aware that what I am writing may actually be what God wants to tell me. I dare to presume that His Spirit is often operative in the things I am choosing to think about and record"** (Gordon MacDonald, *Ordering Your Private World*).

5. ***Record insights.***

**We need to write down how a Scripture suddenly makes sense to us, or that we understand how to behave as God wishes. Writing it reinforces it in our minds and leaves it in place for us to return to if needed.**

**"Truths are inscribed in the heart by the finger of God and remain there firm and indelible. Do not neglect these truths which God inscribes but write them down. And upon writing down the direction one believes God is taking them and acting upon what is written down I have no doubt or reservation to say one will know God's will for their lives"** (From *The Art of Prayer*).

(12-15 minutes)

Experimenting with Journaling

Distribute Resource 17, "Let's Try Journaling," to each group member. Have additional lined paper handy. Read the instructions for the projects together and have each group member choose one of them.

Allow several minutes for people to try journaling. Encourage them to station themselves as far apart as possible in your meeting area for maximum privacy.

Then regather the whole group.

## 4 Take-home Tips

(5-10 minutes)

Discussing How to Journal or Use Other Forms of Expression

Ask group members to choose partners and talk with each other about these two items:

1. How they felt about their journaling experiment. This doesn't necessarily mean sharing what was written since it's private, but sharing their experience in writing it.

2. Nonwritten ways in which they could express themselves to God—woodworking, sketching, listening to music, playing an instrument, etc.

After partners share, you might mention the following journaling tips if time allows.

*Methods for journaling*

There is no one right method, but some people have found these helpful:

• Copying important Bible verses or phrases from Christian books and writing what they mean to you.

- Writing your prayers
- Recording concerns over your own spiritual behavior
- Writing your hopes for the spiritual growth of others, especially family members

*Suggested materials for journaling*

- Spiral notebook (pick the size and weight you prefer)
- A "blank book"
- A special pen or series of colored pens to use according to the mood you're in
- A special place such as a chair or even in bed

Close in prayer, thanking God for all the way we can express ourselves to Him. If you want to prepare the group for next time, distribute copies of Resource 18, "The Case of the Disappearing Majesty." Encourage group members to discuss this idea of "disappearing majesty" with a friend or family member.

# Why Bother to Journal?

## TURN CONFUSION INTO CLARITY

Ken can't tell what he's feeling or thinking sometimes until he writes it down. After a flurry of writing, he rereads his journal and his thoughts finally make sense.

## THINK 'OUT LOUD'

Helen gets tired of driving her husband and friends crazy with her thoughts and feelings. Through the journal, she senses that God is a patient listener as she rambles on.

## REVEAL OUR TRUE SELVES

Martin is serious about overcoming his bad habits, but he won't admit them to fellow Christians. But he does admit them to God on paper and closes with, "If we confess our sins, God is faithful to forgive us."

## LISTEN TO GOD

After Cindy prays, she stops with her pen poised in her hand. She records the thoughts that come into her mind. Then she rereads them to determine whether God might have been speaking to her.

## RECORD INSIGHTS

After working on a problem for days, Jack understands which biblical principle he should have been applying. He writes down these "breakthroughs" so he won't forget them. This way they'll stay in mind—so that he'll realize them sooner next time.

# Let's Try Journaling

## Choose one of the following journaling projects:

**1. Psalm** 42:1-4 *(or another Psalm about how we relate to God).*

**• Personalize it to include you and your struggles and victories, and even specific people and problems in your life.**

**2. I John** 3:16-20 *(or another teaching verse or a meditation from a devotional book).*

**• Write about the struggles and victories you've had obeying this Scripture.**

**3. Mark** 10:17-23 *(or another Gospel narrative).*

**• Imagine yourself as part of this story. Pretend you're the young man or an observer to the situation.**
**How do you feel about Jesus?**
**About what He said?**
**About how He said it?**
**What questions would you have liked to ask Jesus, but you didn't have the courage?**
**Do you have any doubts or private wishes you would have been too afraid to express?**

# The Case of the Disappearing Majesty

> "We must practice the art of long and loving meditation upon the majesty of God. This will take some effort, for the concept of majesty has all but disappeared from the human race."
> —A. W. Tozer

**Why is the idea of worship and majesty so foreign to most Christians in the western hemisphere?**

*Mark the trends below that you think caused this.*

____ Decrease in monarchy-type governments

____ Decrease of respect for public leaders

____ Increase in feelings of personal competence because of the abundance of personal computers and therapists

____ Increase of our culture's feeling of competence because of advances such as space travel

____ Other:

**God plays several roles in our lives, some of which are listed below. Rank these four roles from 1 to 4 with 1 being the role you relate to best.**

____ CREATOR

____ FATHER

____ FRIEND

____ RULER

**Why do you relate to these roles this way?**

# ONE-TO-ONE WORSHIP

## Personal Worship of God

When many people think of worship, they think of doing something in church—mainly singing or reciting. But worship is important in our devotional lives, too. The other components of our devotional lives often bring us spiritually and emotionally to a point at which we want to worship God. Our devotional lives teach us something of God's divine majesty and we want to express it.

This worship is our gift to God, even our performance for Him. He is our divine audience.

Yet personal worship benefits us. It helps prepare us for life. It helps us trust God because we have acknowledged who's in charge. It prepares us for corporate worship at church; no longer does the worship leader have to talk us into worshiping God.

Once again, the Psalms set the tone of this session. They teach us to get beyond our cries for help and come around to celebrating the fact that God reigns.

### Where You're Headed

To help group members feel motivated and equipped to worship in private.

### Scriptures You'll Apply

Psalms 99, 145

### Things You'll Need

- Bibles
- Pens or pencils
- Paper
- Chalkboard and chalk or other display surface
- Hymnals (optional)
- Copies of Resource 19, "Riches to Rags," copied as a transparency or as a handout
- Resource 20, "Worship Starter Kit," copied as a transparency or as a handout
- Overhead projection equipment (optional)
- Copies of Resource 21, "Future Devotional Developments"

## 1 Weak on Worship?

(7-12 minutes)

Looking at How We View Worship

Display or distribute copies of Resource 19, "Riches to Rags." Ask group members to pinpoint where they belong on the chart—closer to the "Throne Room Mentality" or "Going Through the Motions." Have them pick partners and share their answers and reasons.

Next, write the word "majesty" on the chalkboard or elsewhere and ask partners to tell each other the first word or phrase that comes to mind when they see that word.

Then add the words "splendor" and "glory" and ask:

**Which of the these words do you understand most easily in relation to God? Why?**

**What verse or passage in the Bible pictures God's majesty best for you?** (Possibilities: Matthew 17:1-3; Psalm 18:9-15.)

If you have time, read each of the following quotes about worship and have partners tell each other their reactions.

**1. "We have got so commercialized that we only go to God for something from Him, and not for Himself"** (Oswald Chambers, *My Utmost for His Highest*, Barbour and Company, Inc.).

**2. "The act of worship, as carried on by Christians, seems to me to be debasing rather than ennobling. It involves groveling before a Being who, if He really exists, deserves to be denounced instead of respected"** (H. L. Mencken).

**3. "Suppose you are watching a football game and see your favorite athletic hero give a sterling performance.**

**"As you meet him afterwards, you can't help slapping him on the back, putting your arms around him and saying something like, 'It was spectacular the way you caught that pass, then evaded this tackler, stiff-armed that one, ran over this one, got through the last tackle, over the goal line and scored that touchdown.' As you rehearse in his presence what he did, you cannot add to his person or to his performance. You cannot take away from his person or performance. But as you praise his deeds, you are giving glory to him. We need to rehearse in God's presence what we think about the greatness of His Person and the wonder and greatness of all His works"** (Jim Downing, *Meditation*, NavPress).

## 2 How Great Thou Art

(20-25 minutes)

Looking at Specific Aspects of the God We Worship

Before the session, look at Resource 20, "Worship Starter Kit," and choose at least one reference under each of the three headings which you would like the group to examine further.

At this point in the session, display Resource 20 (or distribute copies of it as handouts). Have volunteers look up the passages you chose and note what they say about God's qualities, His greatness and majesty, or His mighty deeds.

With this background complete, assign group members specific psalms or popular hymns (or a combination of both; see suggestions that follow). Ask people to search the Book of Psalms or hymnbooks for God's qualities, for His greatness and majesty, and for His mighty deeds. Distribute blank paper if needed.

Answers will overlap and opinions may differ, but here are some suggested answers.

*Psalm 99*

Qualities: vs. 4

Greatness: vss. 1-3, 5, 9

Deeds: vss. 6-8

*Psalm 145*

Qualities: vss. 8, 9

Greatness: vss. 1-7, 21

Deeds: vss. 10-13

*Hymns*

Qualities: "Great Is Thy Faithfulness"—all verses

Greatness: "A Mighty Fortress"—first half, first verse; second half, second verse

Deeds: "How Great Thou Art"—first, second, and third verses

If time allows, read Hebrews 13:15.

**What do you think it means to "offer a sacrifice of praise"?** (One possibility: To worship even when you have a low sense of the power of God.)

**How do you feel about singing as part of personal worship? Would it seem "weird" to sing by yourself? How is it different from singing in the shower or singing along with the car radio?**

As time allows, share some of the following information on the benefits of using music in worship.

• **"Time spent in singing songs to the Lord about Himself can aid us in knowing the Lord . . . There are relatively few hymns that are songs to the Lord. Most of them are songs about the Lord. It is good to sing songs to the Lord just about Him. This is real worship"** (Frank Minirth and Paul Meier, *Happiness is a Choice*, Baker Book House).

• **Psychologist Janet Lapp of California State University in Fresno trained migraine sufferers to use tranquil music to relax and get rid of headaches. After one year, this group had only one-sixth as many headaches as they'd had before training, and those headaches were less severe and ended more quickly. Lapp guesses that listening to music releases endorphins, the body's natural painkillers** (*Psychology Today*, "Crosstalk," February 1987).

**What if you don't like to sing**? (Singing is just one method of worship. We can also meditate on Scripture about God's majesty; concentrate on God's exemplary qualities; borrow a premier worshiper's words by paraphrasing the Psalms, etc.)

**How is worshiping God different from praising God in prayer?**

As needed, point out that personal worship is not all that different from prayer, except that it may be more expressive; we may sing or even shout or play an instrument as the psalmist did, for instance. This session concentrates on worship separately because worship is emphasized so much in Scripture. Whole chapters of the Old Testament are devoted to mechanics and descriptions of worship. Whole chapters of the Psalms are filled with praise.

## 3 Worship Workout

(10-12 minutes)

Trying Out a Time of Personal Worship

**When is the best time to have personal worship?**

Let people express varying opinions. Then continue:

**Sometimes worship happens in the most unexpected places at the most unexpected times. Take Dennis and Marcy, for instance.**

**Dennis had a flat tire and called the service station to change it because he had on his work clothes. During his hour-long wait, he found a cassette of praise songs in the glove compartment and played them on his battery-powered cassette player. After a while, he couldn't help humming along. The bushes on the side of the freeway began looking more beautiful. There in the midst of gasoline fumes on a highway, God's majesty was real.**

**Marcy's baby has colic, so Marcy spends a lot of time with her baby in a rocking chair in the dark. "Singing soothes the baby, so I sing all the hymns I know by heart," she says. "How different that is from reading them in the hymnal! I really get into it and belt them out."**

Observe that people can look for special occasions to worship, too. For example, they might take advantage of a vacation setting, especially one surrounded by natural beauty. They can arrange to be alone, breathing in the smells and seeing the sights and singing to the Lord.

**Now let's try to have a time of personal worship—right here.**

**Keep your Bible open and sit so you can view the "Worship Starter Kit" sheet. I'll introduce each section (use headings on the sheet). As I do, concentrate on the words on the sheet—or turn to that particular passage and concentrate on it. I'll allow two or three minutes and then mention the second heading. Then I'll do the same with the third.**

Before or after your time of personal worship, you may want to share these tips:

1. Use specific language. Don't just say "Praise You, God." Say exactly what you're praising Him for.
2. Try using the names of God—Rock, Redeemer, Creator, Savior, Prince of Peace, Bread of Life, King of Kings.
3. Use the Scriptures. Quote directly from Psalms if you like, paraphrasing them as if spoken directly to God.
4. Use music—favorite hymns, songs, even recordings by Christian singers.

(adapted from "Learning to Praise," by Barbara Haycraft, *Discipleship Journal*, Issue 38).

# 4

## The Best Is Yet to Come

(12-15 minutes)

Planning How to Change Our Devotional Lives

Distribute copies of Resource 21, "Future Devotional Developments," and ask group members to fill it out. If time permits, form groups of three and discuss the changes participants would like to make.

You may also want to suggest resources like these for further study:

Leslie F. Brandt, *Psalms/Now*, Concordia Publishing House.

Jack R. Taylor, *The Hallelujah Factor*, Broadman Press.

Richard Foster, *Celebration of Discipline*, Harper and Row Publishers, chapters 11 and 13.

Close in prayer, asking God to enrich group members' devotional lives as they seek to know Him better and to enjoy Him more.

# Riches to Rags

## THRONE ROOM MENTALITY

"The perspective of praise is none other than the throne room of the universe where we see God sitting on a throne!"—Jack Taylor (*The Hallelujah Factor*, Broadman Press)

10

9

8

7

6

5

4

3

2

1

## GOING THROUGH THE MOTIONS

"What's so great about worship? At church, we sing songs that I don't understand or that repeat themselves. I don't even like to sing!"

# Worship Starter Kit

## GOD'S QUALITIES

Proverbs 9:10: Wisdom
Psalm 19:1, 4: Creativity
I Peter 3:12, 13: Protection
Psalm 119:64: Unfailing love
Ephesians 2:24, 25: Compassion
Matthew 5:45: Fairness
James 1:17: Generosity

## GOD 'S GREATNESS AND MAJESTY

I Chronicles 29:12
"Wealth and honor come from you; you are the ruler of all things. In your hands are strength and power to exalt and give strength to all."
Psalm 8:1b
"How majestic is your name in all the earth!"
Psalm 99:1b
"He sits enthroned between the cherubim; let the earth shake."
Psalm 113:5
"Who is like the Lord our God, the One who sits enthroned on high."

## GOD'S MIGHTY DEEDS

Psalm 104:5
"He set the earth on its foundations; it can never be moved."
Psalm 105:37
"He brought out Israel, laden with silver and gold, and from among their tribes no one faltered."

# FUTURE DEVOTIONAL DEVELOPMENTS

Here are some attitudes and actions you might choose as a result of this course. Categorize them by writing the corresponding number *(1 through 4)* in the blank before each attitude or action.

**1. TODAY** (I definitely want to do this.)
**2. TOMORROW** (I want to think more about this.)
**3. NEXT YEAR** (I'm not ready to tackle this yet.)
**4. MAYBE NEVER** (I don't like this idea, or I don't think I need it.)

### A. He Loves Me!

_____ Thank God that He loves and accepts me even though my devotional life is not what I'd like it to be.

### B. Confessions of a Bored Bible Reader

_____ Understand the difference between Bible study and devotional Bible reading.

_____ Come to Bible reading with a sense of expectation, instead of a sense of duty.

### C. Soaking in the Scripture

_____ See the value of Christian meditation.

_____ Meditate on God—His unfailing love, His works, His commands, His promises.

### D. Talking with Someone Who Likes You

_____ Have a balanced prayer life—praise, admit, request, thank.

_____ Be honest with God in prayer, expressing my deepest thoughts and desires.

### E. Opening Up to God

_____ See the value of journaling.

_____ Express myself to God by journaling or another activity (woodworking, sketching, ______________________).

### F. One-to-One Worship

_____ Include personal worship in my devotional life.

_____ Have a stronger sense of God's greatness and majesty.